Original title:
The Siren's Breath

Copyright © 2025 Creative Arts Management OÜ
All rights reserved.

Author: Gideon Shaw
ISBN HARDBACK: 978-1-80587-286-3
ISBN PAPERBACK: 978-1-80587-756-1

Currents of Past Regrets

In the depths where laughter hides,
Mermaids giggle, playfully bides.
With every splash of salty brine,
They ask of choices, 'Was it fine?'

A sailor tripped on his old shoe,
Swam with dolphins, what a view!
He forgot his fishnet for the day,
Now he's tangled in seaweed's play.

One winked at him with playful glee,
'You should've listened, not just me!'
But he smiled wide, a rogue at best,
In waters deep, he found his jest.

With each new wave of silly pride,
They tossed back memories, far and wide.
The tide would laugh, the sun would spin,
And in their folly, they'd all win.

Melodies from the Coral Curve

In the depths where the fish do sing,
Bubbles burst with a giggly zing.
Crabs dance in their tiny crew,
Waving claws like they know what to do.

Octopus plays a fiddle blue,
Twirling with joy, it's quite a view.
Seaweed sways in rhythm too,
While the clownfish tell a joke or two.

Secrets Woven in Seafoam

Secrets drift on the salty breeze,
Whispers of how to tease the seas.
Starfish giggle at passing boats,
While schools of fish wear silly coats.

A dolphin's laugh echoes bright,
Mixing laughter with delight.
Seagulls squawk in snarky tones,
Hiding treasure 'neath their stones.

Call of the Enigmatic Waves

Waves come in with a playful crest,
Making splashy jokes at their best.
Turtles glide in silly slow,
With sunglasses on, they steal the show.

Jellyfish jiggle in pastel lights,
Hosting parties on starry nights.
With every bubble, a chuckle flares,
As the ocean fills with funny flares.

Beneath the Surface's Lure

Beneath the waves, the laughter grows,
Where the busy shrimp sneakily pose.
Clownfish paint their faces bright,
Posing for selfies, what a sight!

A sea monster plays peek-a-boo,
Tickling waves like it always do.
With every wave, there's giggles galore,
As the tide rolls in, what's not to adore?

Tidal Whispers of Lost Love

In the frothy waves, I lost my shoe,
Hoping it swam to a lover so true.
Instead, it danced with a fish on a date,
Leaving me here with my lonely fate.

Seagulls laugh as I shout in despair,
Why can't they see? My heart's laid bare!
But they just swoop in for fries from my hand,
While I ponder my love life, clueless and bland.

Haunting Chants In Moonlit Currents

Under the moon, with a wobbly tune,
I serenade fish under starlit gloom.
They bubble with laughter, a watery roar,
While I trip over seaweed, and roll on the floor.

A crab thinks I'm charming, he crabs up to dance,
But my two left fins give him not much a chance.
His exoskeleton snaps as he tries for a twirl,
Leaving me to ponder, is love such a whirl?

Surging Fantasies from Ocean Depths

I dreamed of a merman with hair like the sea,
But underwater styles are hard, you see.
With bubbles and splashes, I made quite a splash,
Only to find my love had turned into trash.

An octopus winked with a mischievous squeeze,
While my heart was tangled like driftwood in reeds.
He offered me pearls, but my eyes turned to goo,
As I slipped on a clam and bid him adieu.

Tranquil Calls of the Briny Deep

Fish tease my dreams with their bubble-filled glee,
They poke fun at me as I swim 'round a tree.
With each silly wave, my laughter does swell,
In the depths of the sea, where seaweed can tell.

A dolphin named Bob makes his rounds with a grin,
Throwing sea snacks at all of my kin.
But as I giggle and wave to the flow,
I trip over barnacles and put on a show.

Melodic Currents in Celestial Harmony

In shimmering waves, fish dance and play,
They argue who leads in this fin-tastic ballet.
A crab with a hat claps claws with delight,
While bubbles of laughter float up to the night.

The shoe of a mermaid is lost in the blue,
A snail is now wearing it, quite proud, it's true.
They giggle and wiggle, spinning round and round,
As shadows of seaweed sway gently, unbound.

Corners of the Watery Realm

In corals that sing, a starfish will twist,
Declaring it's king; 'You'll not be missed!'
Octopus jokers pull pranks on the shore,
With ticklish tendrils, they beg for encore.

A clam held a party, shells stacked up high,
In the corner of reef where the shy fish swim by.
Alligators with tuxes danced waltzes with pride,
While the sea anemones swayed side to side.

Celestial Chords Among Tidal Pools

A jellyfish juggles its glowing bright orb,
While a flatfish tells tales that draw quite a crowd.
A hermit crab shimmies in borrowed attire,
As laughter erupts, they're setting it on fire!

The tide pools compose a sweet symphonic sound,
Sea urchins hum along, wisdom profound.
With each splash and dash, the ocean's alive,
As barnacles giggle, just happy to thrive.

Murmurs from Forgotten Depths

Bubbles release secrets from deep down below,
Where lobsters in tuxedos put on quite a show.
They gather for tales of fishy old lore,
And one little shrimp keeps asking for more.

With winkles and giggles, they plot their next quest,
Sirens on break, they'll forever invest.
In a treasure map drawn on sandy sea beds,
With laughter and joy, they'll follow their threads.

Allure of the Sunset Sea

Waves giggle and splash, oh what a sight,
Seagulls steal fries, then take to flight.
Sunset winks, paints the sky pink,
Mermaids in swimsuits, blink, blink, blink!

Crabs doing the cha-cha on sandy shores,
Jellyfish float by, opening doors.
A fish flips a tail, says 'Look at me!'
While dolphins surf waves, all wild and free.

Serenade in Stormy Skies

Thunder rolls in, a drummer on cue,
Wind sings its tunes, oh what a view.
Umbrellas fly high, like kites in the air,
While fishermen shout, 'Who tied this hair?'

Rain drops a beat, makes puddles so deep,
Ducks don galoshes, splash with a leap.
Lightning takes selfies, all while we laugh,
Nature's own show, no need for a gaffe.

Melodies in the Moonlit Surf

The moon's a big joker, grinning so bright,
Waves hum a tune under soft silver light.
Crickets start clapping, a night-time encore,
While mermaids groan, 'We lost the last score!'

Starfish are dancers, with moves super slick,
Sea turtles chuckle, they get the last kick.
A beach ball rolls in, all covered in sand,
And finds a lost flip-flop, takes a grand stand.

Dance of the Tidal Spirits

Tides tap their toes, a most lively jig,
Seaweed sways softly, sportin' a wig.
Wind whistles tunes that make seashells grin,
While crabs wiggle arms, showing off their skin.

Pelicans strut, with style and flair,
Wishing for snacks, oh where's that fair?
The ocean whispers jokes, listen and see,
Joyfully swirling, wild as can be.

Trance of the Ocean's Heart

On a rock I sat, feeling so spry,
A sea gull cawed, oh my, oh my!
The waves danced close, a splashy affair,
They tickled my toes, what a goofy scare!

Fish nearby giggled with bubbly glee,
Sardines played tag, just like you and me!
The dolphins pranced in a silly delight,
Flipping and flapping, what a crazy sight!

A crab waved his claw, signing a tune,
Tapping his feet to the tidal monsoon.
The seaweed swayed, joined in the fun,
A party at sea, oh wow, we've won!

As the sun dipped low, the hour grew late,
I waved bye to the fish—oh, what a mate!
With laughter and bubbles, I floated away,
In the trance of the ocean, forever to play.

Gift of the Midnight Waves

Under the moonlight, so bright and round,
Fish wear tuxedos, all dresses abound.
The sea whispers secrets, oh what a deal,
Conch shells are giggling; they know how to peel!

The mermaid laughs, her hair all a-swish,
A clam joined in; it made quite a dish!
They feasted on sandwiches made of sea bread,
With jellyfish jam; I can't trust my head!

Starfish played poker; they raised a fin,
While I just sat back, laughing at their grin.
The jellyfish spun like a disco ball,
Underwater craziness, a marvelous hall!

As dawn cracked open, I bid adieu,
To the underwater crew, a salty view.
Next midnight I'll return, with snacks in a sack,
For the ocean's odd party, oh please, take me back!

Reflection in the Brine

I looked in the brine, what a sight to behold,
A fish made a face, so goofy and bold!
He flipped and flopped, showing off his bling,
With scales like diamonds, oh, he could sing!

The octopus waved from his throne made of shells,
Telling me tales of underwater smells.
"Watch out for bubbles," he said with a grin,
"They tickle your nose and make you spit gin!"

A sea turtle joined with a slow-motion dance,
Spinning his shell in a soft, dreamy trance.
The sand squids giggled, their arms in a twist,
Making silly shapes, I had to insist!

As the tide turned low, I waved them goodbye,
My reflection still chuckled, oh me, oh my!
In the brine's silly magic, I found my own cheer,
With undersea friends, I'll always draw near.

Whirlwind of the Tidal Echo

In the whirlwind dance of the tidal swell,
Clams were in cahoots with a wise old snail.
"Join us," they said, "we'll teach you to spin!"
In the ocean's embrace, let the laughter begin!

I tried a few moves, put the sea air in motion,
While crabs called me partner, what a commotion!
They tapped their little feet, all in a row,
While I twirled and whirled, giving it a go!

Anemones clapped, in a colorful show,
Each wave held a rhythm, fast or slow.
Seashells spun tales of days gone by,
With salty confessions and bubbly sighs!

As the sun peeked up, the ocean waved back,
Rolling in laughter, on its watery track.
What a whirlwind journey, so wild and free,
In the tidal echo, just you wait and see!

Tides of Longing and Desire

In ocean's sway, a fish did sing,
With scales that sparkled, a vibrant bling.
She tossed her hair, a silly show,
While seagulls laughed at her wavy flow.

A crab joined in, with his top hat wide,
Attempting dance, with no ocean guide.
He tripped and tumbled, a slapstick scene,
As waves rolled in with a playful sheen.

The starfish giggled from sandy beds,
While jellyfish jiggled, flipping heads.
With every splash, they'd boisterously cheer,
As fishy tales grew with every year.

Sirens in the Twilight Dance

Under the moon, the mermaids prance,
With glittery tails, they lead their dance.
They call for sailors, to join their glee,
But slip on seaweed—oh, what a spree!

A dolphin leaped, made quite the splash,
And everyone giggled at his sudden crash.
"Come here, good sirs, join our merry tune!"
"Just watch your step, or you'll end up marooned!"

With waves of laughter, they splashed and spun,
As sea creatures joined in the crazy fun.
The stars above twinkled and swayed,
While seaweed floated, blissfully laid.

Unfathomable Call of the Depth

In ocean's depths, a voice so clear,
But turned out to be a confused sea steer.
He hummed a tune, completely off key,
Scaring fish away, and tickling the sea.

With barnacles glued to his silly side,
He tried to swim, but he couldn't hide.
The fishes laughed, oh what a sight!
As they danced around him, full of delight.

The octopus joined, with an eight-armed glide,
Wearing old shells like a fashion guide.
"Let's start a band!" they all proclaimed,
With seaweed shakers, they soon were famed.

Harbingers of the Vesper Tide

When twilight falls, the sea creatures scheme,
They gather 'round, devising a dream.
A race on waves with speedboats in tow,
But all went wrong when they started to tow.

The turtles zoomed, the fish gave chase,
But all got tangled in a jiggly race.
With laughs and splashes, they traded a grin,
As eels wrapped 'round, they all took a spin.

With laughter echoing 'neath the pale moon,
The lesson was learned: don't race too soon.
In unison, they sang with glee,
And danced with currents, forever free.

Constellations Tied to the Waves

In a boat, I took a trip,
Singing to fish, they started to flip.
Stars above, they twinkled with glee,
While a crab danced, claiming a tea.

Seagulls squawked, a wild duet,
As I tried to catch dinner, a soggy wet bet.
The waves laughed, splashing all around,
I serenaded dolphins; they hardly made a sound.

A mermaid peeked with a mischievous grin,
Holding a shell, filled with gin.
She offered a sip, I took a brave swig,
Then sang a note, which turned into a jig.

So here I am, on this fine spree,
Caught in a whirlpool of nonsense and glee.
The stars still wink as I float in delight,
Chasing starlit waves through the night.

Whispering Waters in Midnight's Solace

Midnight whispers with a chuckle so deep,
A fish tells secrets as I start to sleep.
Drifting away on a soft, silly tide,
With a sea turtle that rolled like a ride.

Moonlight winks with a playful beam,
My floaty friend, quite the slippery dream.
He jokes about tides with a comical flow,
Riding high waves, way too slow.

Shells sing songs when the twilight hits,
As crabs toast marshmallows and giggle in bits.
The ocean's chorus, a humorous blend,
Keeps the night lively; this party won't end.

Mermaids laugh and do silly flips,
While I sip water from a cup that slips.
So here we float, in this watery jest,
Finding joy in chaos, oh, what a fest!

Lament of the Wind-Tossed Sea

Oh, the sea weeps with a quirky tune,
Dancing waves in the light of the moon.
Wind-tossed laughter, like a raucous cheer,
As octopuses juggle with pint-sized beer.

A fish in a bow tie sings a sharp note,
While seaweed wiggles in a boat that won't float.
Gulls on the sideline, arms crossed in glee,
Point fingers at whales dressed as a tree.

The salty breeze carries jokes in the brine,
As floating sea cucumbers sip on their wine.
Shells cackle loudly, sharing the tales,
Of how one silly crab lost all of its males.

So here in the depths, life's a large jest,
With sharks giving high fives and fish on a quest.
The wind-tossed sea in its whimsical sway,
Reminds us to laugh as we dance through the day.

Bubbles of Distant Yearnings

Bubbles rise up, with secrets to tell,
Of fish who get lost, in a coral shell.
They float like balloons, dreaming of land,
While barnacles giggle at plans that are bland.

An octopus waves to a clueless old whale,
"Why swim in circles? Let's set a new trail!"
The sea bubbles burst with a giggling sound,
As jellyfish shimmy like they've just found.

Distant yearnings twist in the foam,
While waves plot mischief like a new home.
They whisper sweet nothings to wayward boats,
As mermaids hum songs of adventurous quotes.

So lift up a shell, and hear what they sing,
Of how much they love a jellybean fling.
With bubbles of laughter, so light and so free,
Life under the waves is a grand mystery!

Siren's Embrace in Velvet Seas

In velvet waves, a giggle plays,
Where mermaids dance and dolphins graze.
A fish with shoes prances on sand,
While crabs gather 'round to form a band.

Tales of treasure hide in jest,
With seaweed hats, they look their best.
Octopus holds a cocktail glass,
As sea cucumbers join the sass.

The gulls squawk loud, a laughter shoot,
While turtles wear their favorite suit.
Jellyfish float like disco balls,
Inviting all to dance in thralls.

So come aboard this merry ride,
Where every wave is filled with pride.
Embrace the splash, let worries cease,
Dive into this world of silly peace.

Songs of Shores Unknown

In distant lands where crabs go bold,
The seashells sing tales yet untold.
With every gust, a giggle flies,
As fish wear hats that block the skies.

Pirates hide from goofy rays,
Claiming goldfish in a laugh-filled blaze.
Sailing boats made out of cheese,
With creamy sails that dance in ease.

A whale tells jokes, and dolphins chuckle,
As seagulls play in frothy puddles.
With sand stacked high in quirky shapes,
The beach becomes a realm of gapes.

So let's explore those shores unknown,
Where silly songs make hearts feel grown.
In the waves, find joy and cheer,
With laughter echoing far and near.

Fantasies Cradled in Salt and Foam

In salty foam, dreams start to swirl,
With starfish twirls and seaweed curls.
A clam takes a nap in a hammock swing,
While lobsters joke about everything!

Seashells whisper plans for the day,
In a world where fish know how to sway.
Balloons made of bubbles drift high,
Tickling the pink clouds in the sky.

Anemones play hide and seek,
With octopuses getting cheeky and sleek.
They trade silly hats for scented breeze,
And dance out loud with goofy ease.

So laugh along with waves that tease,
While crabs sip soda beneath swaying trees.
In a realm where giggles have a home,
Join the party, let your spirit roam.

Sighs of the Ocean's Heart

In the depths where shadows do sigh,
The fish share jokes while seahorses fly.
With a wink, the octopus decrees,
"Let's have a party, swim and freeze!"

The waves break out in fits of fun,
As dolphins leap under the sun.
A crab in shades struts in delight,
Saying, "This is the dance of the night!"

With sea anemones in a line,
Twisting and twirling, they shine divine.
The laughter sings through salt-kissed air,
In this wacky world, there's joy to spare.

So gently breathe in the laughter bright,
As waves of humor wash in and recite.
Embrace the quirks of ocean's chart,
Where every splash reveals the heart.

The Lure of Siren's Silver Voice

There's a song in the breeze, oh so sweet,
Sailors dance to a tune on repeat.
Fish are laughing, they join in,
While mermaids giggle, let the fun begin.

Waves are clapping in rhythmic delight,
Seagulls are shouting, 'What a night!'
Every note's a splash, a silly splurge,
When sailors fall in, that's the real urge!

Nearby rocks, they shake and roll,
A seaweed band starts to patrol.
No one can resist, they dive with glee,
Chasing a tune that's so wobbly!

Underwater ballet, fishes in a row,
They flutter their fins in the joyous flow.
Life's a giggle when the ocean sings,
Laughter and bubbles, oh, what it brings!

Crescendo of Celestial Currents

In the waves, a chuckle rides high,
As jellyfish seem to float and sigh.
A plankton party beneath the moon,
They shimmy and shake to a silly tune.

Currents swirl, it's a dance so grand,
Octopuses twirl, just like they planned.
Turtles groove, they take a dip,
Join the fun, let's take a trip!

Under the stars, laughter does shine,
Eels and crabs form a conga line.
Fish flip-flop with a splash so bright,
Underwater revelry through the night!

When the tide rises, the giggles soar,
Mermaids pop up, "Come on, let's explore!"
Nature's symphony, a comic spree,
Sing with the waves, wild and free!

Resonance of the Timeless Sea

The ocean hums a comical tune,
With sea cows mooing under the moon.
Waves wiggle, they make a splash,
As crabs laugh out in a clumsy dash.

Dolphins leap with a flip and twirl,
Making waves in a dancing whirl.
The wind joins in, a jokester too,
Whistling tunes like a playful crew!

Coral reefs giggle with colors bright,
Seaweed sways, feeling so light.
Every echo is filled with cheer,
In this vast world, let's all draw near!

Under the surface, the jokes abound,
A treasure of laughter always found.
With every ripple, we join the fun,
Life in the sea is never done!

Harmony of Whispered Fates

Deep in the surf, secrets are spilled,
Fish with issues, all are thrilled.
Anemones giggle as they sway,
Sharing tales of the silliest day!

Tides are tickling the sandy shore,
Starfish chuckle, wanting more.
Shells conspiracize with a wink or two,
Crafting schemes, what shall we do?

The kelp dances with rhythms so bright,
Married to the wind, it's a comic sight.
Whales hum jokes that echo far,
As sea urchins cheer from afar!

With every wave, the laughter flows,
Whispers of joy in every close.
In this watery world, come join the fun,
We'll sing and dance till the day is done!

Charm of the Forgotten Isles

In waters deep, where treasures sleep,
A fish once wore a hat, oh dear!
His scales, they shone, with mismatched tones,
He danced in circles, full of cheer.

Among the seaweed, jokes were shared,
A crab with claws that clapped and snapped,
He told of tales, of mermaid scales,
While fishfolk laughed, and seashells clapped.

A gull flew by, with a wink and sly,
He snagged a snack, then dropped it flat,
A splash of sauce, it looked like loss,
Yet all just giggled, and that was that!

In isles of mirth, where joy gave birth,
The ocean's tunes, like silly tunes,
With every wave, a laugh to save,
In salty air, life's never prunes!

Embrace of the Salted Wind

A parrot squawked, a comment mocked,
His jokes flew high, they spread their wings,
As sailors blushed, their faces flushed,
   The salty breeze played silly things.

A whale once wore a bowtie neat,
He flipped and flopped, a sight to see,
The dolphins cheered, everyone jeered,
   With splashes made of pure glee.

On ship's deck wide, as waves collide,
The crew slipped on a slippery flip,
With a hearty laugh, they lost their path,
   But never missed a fellow ship!

The winds would play, chase blues away,
   With every gust, laughter arose,
An ocean's jest, at its very best,
   In salted air, joy freely flows!

Enigma of the Aqua Realm

In depths where bubbles dance and sway,
A squid wore glasses, so absurd!
He read the sea, philosophically,
And inked out poems quite unheard.

Eels had fun, with webs they spun,
Creating frights that clashed with lights,
They'd crack a grin, as fish swam in,
To duck and dodge those slippery sights.

Octopus tangled in vibrant threads,
While stars above made dramatic spreads,
He juggled shells, while laughter swells,
A show of cheers from fishy beds!

The coral laughed, like little staff,
Tickled by bubbles, bright with glee,
The magic spun, in every pun,
In aqua realms, so wild and free!

Twilight beneath the Surface

As dusk arrived, the shadows thrived,
A fish in a tux, too snug, too tight,
He tripped and spun, their laughter fun,
In twilight's grip, what a sight!

The rocks were dressed in glittered best,
While clams held court with silly fights,
They moaned and groaned, like squishy phones,
Beneath the stars, the ocean lights.

A stingray flew like a comical view,
With moves so slick, it graced the floor,
The seaweed swayed, in this parade,
As fish joined in, to ask for more!

Once twilight dims, the laughter swims,
In playful waves, where fun resides,
The surface glows, with secret flows,
In depths of night, the joy collides!

Shimmering Shadows of the Coast

Beneath the waves, a fish does dance,
In flippers bright, it takes a chance.
With bubble-lips, it tries to sing,
But sounds like a cat—what a funny thing!

Jellyfish wear the latest trends,
In disco lights, they twist, they bend.
With each slap-slap of tentacle swish,
They dream they're chefs, making jellyfish dish!

Seagulls squawk with a grand parade,
They steal my fries; I'm not afraid!
With sassy struts and eye on a fry,
They show their flair—oh my, oh my!

A sea turtle, slow as a train,
Admires a crab, who struts in vain.
With mismatched socks, they laugh and grin,
In shimmering shadows, let the fun begin!

Allure of Distant Shores

A lighthouse keeper's on a quest,
To find his socks—he's truly blessed!
The tide rolls in with a giant smile,
And waves his hat—it floats a while!

A dolphin jumps, a fishy fling,
It thinks it's a pro, tries to bling-bling.
With mismatched pearls, it strikes a pose,
In undersea fashion, it surely knows!

Sandcastles rise like towering dreams,
But then the tide whispers, 'Oh, it seems…'
With a big belly laugh, they tumble down,
And the crab takes a bow, wearing a crown!

Seashells hold gossip of tales so grand,
With secrets told on the golden sand.
A hermit crab tales a new shell try,
But ends up stuck—oh me, oh my!

Depths Where Dreams Swim

In the deep blue, a puffer fish,
Puffs up big, oh what a wish!
A color clash, it looks absurd,
"Fancy me?" it says, but no one heard!

A clam hums a tune, with such great flair,
But a fish swims close; it starts to stare.
"Please stop that noise," the clam does plead,
But the fish just giggles, 'I'll take the lead!'

Octopus in shades, so suave, so cool,
Displays his tricks in a watery pool.
With eight long limbs showing off his groove,
He dances a jig that makes the fish move!

A whale sings low, with a rumbling laugh,
While seaweed floats, it joins the path.
Bubbles rise up with jokes to share,
In underwater giggles, who wouldn't care?

Maritime Melancholy

A crab with dreams of being a star,
Wears sunglasses while strumming a guitar.
With shell-shock humor, he tells a tale,
About a fish that always turned pale!

Gulls fly by, making quite the scene,
Chasing after snacks, oh what a routine!
With fluttering wings and raucous sounds,
They steal the fisherman's bait—what clown bounds!

An old ship's anchor groans with pride,
While barnacles make it their bumpy ride.
"Once I was grand, now I just glow,"
Sighs the anchor with a wise, salty flow!

But amidst the grumbles of ocean's jest,
There's laughter abounding, it's simply the best.
With bubbles and giggles, they drift and play,
In the maritime mischief, they find their way!

Ebb and Flow of Forgotten Lore

In ocean's sway, they dance and play,
With fishy tales that drift away.
They giggle loud, what a sight to see,
Telling secrets of the deep blue sea.

With bubbles blown and laughter shared,
They plot mischief, none are scared.
In tides of whimsy, they do roam,
While sailors ponder, 'Where's my home?'

Whispers of snacks, a feast awaits,
Shiny trinkets, not far from gates.
They snack on pearls and giggle bright,
As fishermen snore under the starlight.

So here's a toast to those who tease,
The ocean's jesters that aim to please.
In every wave, a chuckle's found,
In the ebb and flow, just silly sound.

Serenade of the Forgotten Depths

In forgotten depths, a tune does flow,
Of ticklish toes in the undertow.
They strum on seaweed; it squeaks and squeals,
As crabs join in with their tiny meals.

An octopus wears a tiny hat,
While jellyfish glide with a friendly spat.
They harmonize, with fish on keys,
Creating melodies that waft on breeze.

With every note, they swirl and spin,
The squids get wiggly, a playful din.
In the deep blue, they laugh and jive,
As tides of joy help them thrive.

Oh, sing with glee in watery halls,
Where sea life dances and friendship calls.
For in the depths where laughter reigns,
The chorus of the ocean, it never wanes.

Nautical Dreams and Moonlit Hopes

Under the moon, dreams sail on high,
With twinkling stars, they wink and sigh.
Boats filled with giggles, laughter so sweet,
In whimsical waves, they gather and meet.

They toast with seashells, clink and cheer,
As the tides of joy pull them near.
In realms of tightrope fishy fun,
Splashing and laughing, oh what a run!

With nautical maps drawn on sand,
They plot their journeys hand in hand.
Each wave a tale, each ripple a smile,
To ride life's currents, what's worth the while.

So chase the tides, let your heart sail,
With a sprinkle of joy, you cannot fail.
In nautical dreams, let laughter unfurl,
As moonlit hopes dance and twirl.

Melodies That Make the Heart Drift

With tunes that tumble like ocean spray,
The heart drifts off in a silly way.
A merry mermaid with a ukulele,
Sings to the fish, "Let's have a daily!"

The gulls join in with chorus so bright,
As barnacles tap and crustaceans bite.
In bubbles of laughter, they sway and twirl,
Dancing along in a watery whirl.

With a splash of whimsy and echoes of fun,
Every note pulls at the strings, we're spun.
They spin with joy like a fishy ballet,
Making hearts smile in their own special way.

So let the melodies carry you far,
With giggles and grins like a sea-bound star.
In rhythms of joy, let the heart drift free,
As oceanic laughter writes history.

Beneath the Veil of Water

Bubbles pop like candy rain,
Fish wear smiles, it's quite insane.
Mermaids giggle, flip their tails,
Singing songs of tangled trails.

Jellyfish dance in wild delight,
While seahorses hold a kite.
Coral reefs join in the fun,
Underneath the water's run.

Starfish try to bake a pie,
Clams compete in who can fly.
Octopus serves drinks on cue,
In the bar where all's askew.

Down below, the laughter swells,
Amidst the swaying seaweed bells.
Join the party, take a dive,
In the depths, we come alive!

Siren's Caress Under Starlit Skies

In the twilight, shadows play,
Whales attempt a ballet sway.
Nautical snacks are served with flair,
As dolphins giggle in midair.

A sea cucumber's fashion show,
With starfish strutting, stealing the glow.
Nothing compares to this wild ride,
With winks and waves from the ocean's tide.

Clownfish crack jokes and spin tales,
As turtles share their underwater sails.
Crabs do cartwheels, oh what a sight,
Under the moon's sparkling light!

Here in this realm, laughter reigns free,
As sea creatures dance just for glee.
Join the fun, forget your woes,
Beneath the stars, anything goes!

Currents of Eternal Enchantment

Currents twist with magic flair,
Eels prank each other without a care.
A stingray glides with a cheeky grin,
As fish catch jokes on a whim.

Underwater disco, lights flash bright,
Urchins bust moves, such a sight!
With a splash and a dive, fun brings delight,
As the sea's creatures savor the night.

Pufferfish puff, trying to impress,
While crabs critique in fancy dress.
Anemones laugh, swaying in delight,
At the silliness floating in sight.

With bubbles and giggles, the party expands,
Seashells tap dance, following commands.
Join the flow, let worries disperse,
In this world, every laugh's a verse!

Seafaring Secrets of the Heart

Sailors whisper of treasures bright,
While goldfish gossip in the moonlight.
A parrotfish paints tales of bold,
With stories of adventures untold.

Walruses wear oversized hats,
Regaling tales of their acrobats.
A crab debater squabbles with flair,
As lobsters join in, plotting their lair.

Mermaid *Mimi* drops her seashell phone,
Just to catch up with a tuna known.
Unexpected friendships start to form,
As sea cucumbers dance with charm.

In these depths, camaraderie thrives,
With every splash, true joy arrives.
Join the crew on this wavy ride,
With laughter and tales, side by side!

Lullabies of the Ocean's Heart

In a sea of chips and dips,
Fish swim with silly flips.
Seaweed dances in the tide,
Crabs in hats take a ride.

Jellyfish wear rubber shoes,
Sipping on the ocean's booze.
Clams play cards beneath the sun,
What a party, oh what fun!

Starfish telling knock-knock jokes,
Waves are laughing at the folks.
Barnacles with their thick shell
Join the dance and raise some hell!

Seagulls swooping with flair and grace,
Trading tales of silly space.
The ocean's heart beats wild and free,
In laughter's tune, we'll always be.

Siren's Song in Solitude

A lonely rock with a cheeky grin,
Sings to fish where the fun begins.
Bubbles burst with giggles loud,
While octopuses dance, so proud.

Turtles wear shades, and whales take flight,
Surfing waves through the starry night.
In solitude, they sing so bright,
Their joyful tunes are pure delight!

The seafoam laughs at a starfish bling,
And jellyfish join their zany swing.
They spin and twirl through salty air,
Creating magic, beyond compare!

Oh, what a sight, these silly sights,
Mirth flows deep in ocean nights.
With every splash and every cheer,
The water sings, and friends draw near.

Chants of the Deep Unseen

The deep is filled with laughter's call,
The shrimp throw a party that's not so small.
Seahorses bounce on a colorful wave,
As conch shells whistle, bold and brave.

Eels in shades of polka-dot,
Engage in yoga in their little spot.
Mollusks munch on festive treats,
While sea urchins tap their tiny feet.

Sand dollars sing with a twinkling sound,
Stars twirl in rhythm all around.
With bubbles floating, joining the tune,
The ocean's giggle feels like a boon!

Tide pools ripple with bright display,
Nautical nonsense runs into play.
These chants of joy in depths below,
Deliver smiles wherever they go.

Lurking Beneath Starlit Waters

Beneath the stars, where shadows creep,
An octopus jokes, losing sleep.
With eight-legged flair, they wiggle and wave,
What a sight in the night, oh how they rave!

Crab scouts mingle with their best mates,
Finding treasures on sandy plates.
Hidden giggles echo and flow,
The ocean's pranksters, putting on a show!

Bubbles rising with tales so grand,
Fish spin around in a slapstick band.
As the moon chuckles, bringing good cheer,
They share their secrets for all to hear.

In starlit waters, laughter is found,
With glimmering joy all around.
So if you peek beneath the blue,
You'll find a party, just for you!

Tides of Enchantment

A fish tried to sing, what a scene,
But scales and notes just don't convene.
He flopped and flailed, a splashy dance,
Appeased a crab, who took a chance.

The starfish laughed, it rolled with glee,
"Your voice is weaker than seaweed tea!"
The clam just snickered, kept to its shell,
While dolphins giggled, plotting their swell.

In bubbles they whispered, tales of the deep,
"Ha, who knew fishy could try to leap?"
Yet on the tidal stage, all made a splash,
With joy and laughter, it turned quite brash.

So crank up the sea, let the ocean sing,
For fish can't carry a tune, but they bring
The depths of humor, a watery jest,
In currents of fun, we find the best.

Resonance of the Ocean's Kiss

Mermaids have parties, fins in the air,
With crabby DJs and seaweed flair.
The octopus juggles, what a delight,
While seahorses waltz through the shimmering night.

A clam cracks jokes, with pearls of wisdom,
"Why don't starfish play cards? They can't find a system!"
Laughter erupts, echoing broad,
As fish break dance, in pods they applaud.

A whale on the mic, with a voice deep and loud,
Sings about bubbles, the anthem of the crowd.
"When life gives you tides, don't swim against flow,
Just ride the wave, and let humor grow!"

So under the waves, let mirth be the rule,
With laughter and joy, we'll all be the cool.
For even in depths, where shadows once bristled,
A glee-filled ocean will always be whistled.

Whispers of Enchanted Tides

Underwater whispers, a gossiping school,
"The jellyfish stings? Nah, it's just a drool!"
They chuckle and scamper, in coraline hues,
While the sea turtle muses, "Let's party with blues!"

Seagulls above, with sass in the breeze,
Stealing the fish fries, oh what a tease!
The dolphins are diving, all slick and sly,
Casting shellfish glances, oh my, oh my!

In seaweed garlands, they toast with a cheer,
"Here's to the tides and the fish with no fear!"
With fins, they sway, an aquatic ballet,
Spreading the joy, in watery display.

So listen for giggles, if you dive and splish,
For the ocean is full of a whimsical wish.
And while shores may whisper, in night's gentle leap,
The waves hold the secrets the sea creatures keep.

Echoes in the Moonlit Abyss

In the moonlit depths, where shadows play,
A lobster tells tales, but they twist, they sway.
"I once met a fish with a fabulous fin,
He swam like a dragon, but couldn't begin!"

The sea cucumbers snicker, rolling about,
"Dear friend, your jokes are just loony, no doubt!"
While fishes prance round, like stars in the dark,
Creating wild ripples, playing the lark.

The waves hum a tune, a melody neat,
As clams drop the bass, bringing down the beat.
"Let's throw a rave, make a splash in the night,
With currents that dance and blow bubbles so light!"

So join in the frolic, let laughter arise,
From the depths of the ocean, humor flies.
For in this abyss, where shadows entwine,
We swim with a grin and make humor divine!

Secrets of the Seafoam

In bubbles and giggles the fishies sing,
A frolicsome chorus, oh what joy they bring!
The octopus winks with eight cheeky eyes,
While starfish do cartwheels, oh what a surprise!

The seaweed's a wig for the crab's funny head,
He struts like a model, as if he's well-fed.
Giant clams giggle as oysters play chase,
While seahorses dance in a wiggly race!

The jellyfish float with a fluttery grace,
As dolphins and gulls join the undersea chase.
"Come join our party!" the mermaids do cheer,
With bubble gum bubbles, they spread holiday cheer!

But watch for the whale, oh, he thinks he's a clown,
He'll splash with a belly flop, oh how they frown.
As the tide rolls in with a splash and a glint,
Fish laugh till they cry, at that big blubbery stint!

Echoing Hearts of the Deep

Down where the kelp sways and giggles take flight,
Creatures exchange jokes through the soft ocean light.
A grouper tells puns that are quite off the scales,
While crabs are the jesters adorned with their tails.

A clam with a pearl says, "I'm rich as can be!"
"I'll start a showdown with a fish from next sea!"
But the fish just swim by with a wink in their fins,
"Your riches are jokes, my shellfishous friends!"

The shark just rolls eyes at the silly sea pranks,
As turtles breakdance and give five gold ranks.
"Let's conga with currents, and shimmy with zest!"
They spin and they twirl, oh they're simply the best!

But then, from the shadows, a grumpy old eel,
Shakes his great head, "What's the deal with this reel?
You think this is funny? Give me something real!"
So, they catch him a tuna, now that's a great meal!

Shade of the Undersea Queen

In the shadowy depths where the light barely glows,
Lives a queen with a crown made of glittering prose.
With a smile of shells and laughter of pearls,
She winks at the shrimp and makes all their swirls.

Her throne is a shipwreck that no one will claim,
"Let's party!" she shouts, "I'm the queen of this game!"
With a flick of her tail, she calls forth the fun,
Merfolk in a line, they're all ready to run!

A blowfish performs, puffed up with great pride,
While anglerfish glow like the world's funniest guide.
The sea cucumbers roll, and they laugh without shame,
"Who knew being weird would bring us such fame?"

But lurking in darkness, the laughter attracts,
A grumpy old squid whose humor relax.
"Join in the fun or I'll tickle you silly,
With ink and with giggles, oh boy, what a frilly!"

Harmonies of the Water's Edge

Where the ocean and laughter tumble and sway,
Seashells compose melodies night and day.
With a strum of a starfish, and claps from a crab,
The concert of bubbles soon turns into fab!

The pelicans swoop and try out their dance,
While little fish giggle, they just want a chance.
"Sing us a song!" they all chant and they cheer,
But the gulls are too busy to come back down here!

"Let's harmonize waves!" says a flounder so brave,
While dolphins do flips in the aqua-blue wave.
With bubbles like cymbals, the chorus is bright,
As clownfish throw colors in pure delight!

Then a curious seal pops his head from the foam,
"How 'bout a beach ball? Let's party at home!"
So the waves crash a rhythm, and under the sun,
The water's edge echoes with laughter and fun!

Low Tide Musings

As the seaweed twirls with glee,
Crabs dance like they're at a spree.
Fish wear hats, oh what a sight,
Splashing water, pure delight.

Sea cucumbers think they're cool,
While starfish play the fool in the pool.
But jellyfish float by in style,
Winking with a squishy smile.

Seagulls squawk like they're in a band,
With a clam shell making a stand.
The tide rolls in, takes back its throne,
Leaving behind a treasure zone.

So let's skip rocks, make a wish,
Join in on this oceanic dish!
With laughter carried on the tide,
Fun awaits where waves reside.

Elysian Harmonies Underwater

In coral castles where fish play tunes,
Tiny seahorses dance under moons.
Octopuses juggle with hats on their heads,
While turtles roll by on cozy beds.

The hermit crab has quite the news,
He's got a new shell, in funky hues!
"Watch me scoot!" he boasts with pride,
As his shell glimmers with every glide.

A dolphin pokes his head to say,
"Who needs land? I'll surf all day!"
With waves of laughter echoing bright,
Underwater shenanigans, what a sight!

Bubbles rise with giggles and cheer,
As fish invite everyone near.
Join in the fun, let's be free,
In this watery world, just you and me!

Veils of Enchantment Upon the Shore

On sandy beaches, dreams are spun,
As crabs play tag, oh what fun!
Seashells whisper secrets low,
While starfish join in with a show.

The moonlit waves are in a race,
Turtles surf with a smiling face.
Seagulls with their sassy calls,
Waddle through the tide, take falls.

Mermaids swap their tales for laughs,
As seaweed twirls like fancy staffs.
With every splash, a giggle flows,
In this enchanted night, anything goes!

So let's gather around the driftwood fire,
With seafood snacks, let's never tire.
For with each tide that dances ashore,
Adventure awaits, let's explore more!

Siren's Echo Through Brine and Stone

Echoes linger in salty air,
Where dolphins mime and fish do stare.
A barnacle chorus sings down low,
While seaweed sways to the show.

With shells for hats and laughter wide,
Each wave carries joy with the tide.
Mussels gossip, "Did you see?,"
As clams begin to disagree.

The ocean's guffaw fills the beach,
With funny tales just out of reach.
Driftwood sitters, onlookers keen,
Snack on popcorn, a seaside scene.

So let the waves tickle your toes,
In this silly world where fun only grows.
With laughter ringing through brine and stone,
Every smile tells you, you're never alone!

Between the Waves of Solace

Bubbles rise with every laugh,
Fishes giggle in the half.
Seashells tell tales, oh so bright,
As mermaids dance, a comical sight.

Gulls squawk jokes, they never drop,
While crabs moonwalk, ready to bop.
Tides tickle toes, a playful tease,
They beckon you to join with ease.

Beach balls bounce on waves that swell,
The ocean's jest, do you know it well?
Flip-flops flop in splendid cheer,
With giggles echoing far and near.

Let's ride the surf of jolly waves,
Find humor in the ocean's braves.
For every splash, a hearty grin,
In the sea's embrace, we all win!

Silent Serenade of the Tide

The waves hum softly like a tune,
They tickle beaches, morning to noon.
Each drop a note, the ocean plays,
While sunsets blush in laughing rays.

Starfish gossip, oh so sly,
As sea cucumbers wave goodbye.
The dance of kelp, so unrefined,
Makes even the strongest fish reclined.

Otters juggle clams with glee,
Turning dinner into comedy.
Seagulls wheel in aerial roars,
Trading barbs as they soar.

In this serenade, chaos reigns,
The tide's heartbeat, full of gains.
With every wave, let's raise a cheer,
For the humor that lives in here!

Alluring Shadows of the Abyss

In the depths where shadows play,
The fish wear hats in a quirky way.
Jellyfish jiggle as they glide,
Dancing through the ocean wide.

An octopus blends in with style,
Throwing ink with a charming smile.
Seaweed sways to some bass line,
While eels crack jokes on flat design.

Pirates' ghosts share tales of cheer,
With old shipwrecks lingering near.
They throw a bash beneath the waves,
Where laughter echoes, and joy saves.

As bubbles burst with laughter's sound,
In the abyss, fun's always found.
In watery depths, the spirits sing,
Of jests and japes that joy can bring!

Ghosts of the Deep's Melody

Haunted seas play a quirky tune,
With mermaids giggling at the moon.
Anchored ships sway, a jolly crew,
As ghostly shapes glide on through.

The blowfish puffs up in surprise,
While clams share secrets under skies.
Each wave a chuckle from the brine,
The ocean's whispers align just fine.

Anemones dance, lost in a trance,
As sea turtles spin in a slow prance.
Ghosts of sailors, with hearts so light,
Join the party with all their might.

So raise your glass, let laughter ring,
In the depths where merriment springs.
The melody floats, like a memory,
Of playful ghosts in the sea, carefree.

Spellbound by Ocean's Depths

Down in the waves where the fish like to dance,
A mermaid popped up with a mischievous glance.
She sang to the sailors, with a giggle and swish,
"Fool me once, boys, and you'll be my next dish!"

Their boats spun around like a whirlpool of fun,
Each captain was caught in a game to be won.
"With treasure and trinkets, can you find my delight?"
While they tripped on the ropes, she vanished from sight!

Oh, laughter erupted as they splashed about,
"Where are you going?" they shouted, no doubt.
The ocean just chuckled, with waves rolling high,
While the mermaid just winked, watching the crew cry!

In the end they all splashed, declared it a win,
With tales of her charm and the mess they were in.
But the ocean just smiled, with her secrets to keep,
As she rolled with the tide, her laughter was deep!

Reverie of the Fleet-Footed Fish

In a shoal of bright fish, fanciful they glide,
Each one with a tail that's taken a ride.
With nimble little fins, they spin and they twirl,
Chasing seashells and laughter as they swirl!

A crab with a hat joined the playful affair,
He 'cracked' up the jokes, none could compare!
"Why did the fish cross the ocean so wide?"
"To school with the dolphin for a fun waterslide!"

And the dolphins all chuckled, in a splashy ballet,
While the fish made a splash in a bright colored array.
With bubbles and giggles in a watery race,
Each flip and each wiggle set the pace!

So raise a glass, friends, to this feast of delight,
As fish serve their punchlines while swimming in sight.
They'll prank you all day, in their blue ocean quest,
For laughter's the treasure they love the best!

Mirage in the Dappled Light

Beneath the bright surface where the sun likes to play,
A shadow swims by with a smile, quite gay.
"Do you see what I see?" a fish calls to his mate,
"Or is that just seaweed? I can't navigate!"

With bubbles and giggles, they swim through the haze,
A jellyfish wobbles in a glimmering daze.
"What's the fastest way to catch a swift wave?"
"Just follow the light where the giggling ones rave!"

"Oh look at that sparkle!" the fishes all squeal,
"Let's chase after it, what a fantastic deal!"
But when they get closer, it's just a smooth rock,
Leaving them tickled by their tricky sea clock!

And as the sun sets with a wink in its gaze,
They'd dance in the shadows, in a shimmering craze.
For the ocean is full of such mirth and delight,
Where laughter and wonder play tag in the light!

Rapture of the Rolling Swell

Waves rolled in clumsily, like ducks on a quest,
Each crest had a giggle, each trough was a jest.
"Hold on to your fins!" a voice called with cheer,
"Let's ride this swell, there's nothing to fear!"

The sea cucumbers cheered, swaying to and fro,
As the sea urchins laughed at the tide's mighty show.
A whale jumped for joy, making splashes so grand,
While the fish wore their shades, sunbathing on sand!

"Why does the wave break? Is it tired or mad?"
"Oh no!" said the clam, "it's just gone shopping, lad!"
Came back with some seashells and jellyfish bling,
"The ocean's a closet, come see what I bring!"

So they marveled together at this whimsical game,
As the sea's laughter echoed—a joyous refrain.
Through foam and through bubbles, their spirits would swell,
To dance with the tide in a rapture so swell!

Underwater Echoes of Desire

In the depths where fishies sing,
A seaweed dance, oh what a fling!
Bubbles rise with secret dreams,
While lobsters plot in stealthy schemes.

Jellyfish float with graceful flair,
A crush on crabs, they just don't care.
With every splash and giggle loud,
The ocean's quirks draw the crowd.

Whales crack jokes, the dolphins roar,
Mermaids giggle, craving more.
They prank the sharks with a wink and dash,
As fish in tuxedos make a splash!

Anemones wave like they're on stage,
In this underwater circus, they'll engage.
With clams and oysters, laughter flows,
In this world beneath, where anything goes.

Fables from the Ocean Floor

A clam tells tales of the grand sea fair,
With golden pearls and finned debonair.
Octopus chefs whip up fishy stew,
While an eel snores in a cozy shoe.

Seahorses trot like they're in a race,
Chasing each other, full of grace.
Starfish compete with a twisty spin,
All of them giggling, let the feast begin!

Coral reefs echo with stories bright,
Mermaids fashion crowns, oh what a sight!
They crown the fish with colors bold,
As tales of mischief in waves unfold.

A turtle drags his friend so slow,
While the colorful parrotfish put on a show.
With every bubble, laughter spreads wide,
In this underwater realm of joy and pride.

Rhapsody of the Timid Waves

The waves tiptoe with a giggly glee,
Splashing softly, just wait and see!
They whisper secrets of salty dreams,
As fish play hopscotch in silver beams.

Tiny crabs practice their dance,
With wobbly moves that make you prance.
A starfish tells a corny joke,
And all the guppies start to poke.

Seagulls squawk with tons of sass,
While a dolphin plays a seaweed bass.
The horizon dances, oh what fun,
As starry nights make the ocean run!

Hidden treasures in sand so light,
Where clams play catch, oh what a sight.
In flappy fun, they lose their cares,
In a rhapsody of water affairs.

Glistening Chimeras of the Sea

A fish with legs does wobbly prance,
While seahorses join in a silly dance.
Octopuses wear hats, oh what a thrill,
Flaunting their style with uncanny skill.

Merfolk chuckle at tales of surprise,
As sea cucumbers act wise and shy.
They spice up the currents with vibrant tales,
While playful shadows hide in gales.

Crabs in tuxedos bow with finesse,
Freestylin' dolphins, making a mess.
Turtles roll with laughter galore,
While waves still giggle, begging for more.

Underneath stars, the ocean glows,
In quirky dreams, where mischief flows.
With glistening chimeras full of delight,
The underwater party dances all night.

Ballad of the Brave Seafarer

A sailor set forth with a song on his lips,
His ship made of paper, imagined in scripts.
With a hat made of fish, he danced on the waves,
Chasing the echoes of dolphins in caves.

His crew was a flock of very fine ducks,
They quacked to the rhythm, oh, what silly luck!
Together they searched for treasure and gold,
But found only seaweed, it was rather bold.

He shouted, 'Where's my treasure, oh, glorious sea?'
The fish rolled their eyes and said, 'Can't you see?
The best jewels are laughter and friendship so true,
Now go grab a sandwich, there's one just for you!'

They feasted and laughed, the ducks waddled with glee,
Sailing on dreams, wild and always carefree.
The ocean, a jester, with waves that tease,
A dance full of fun, with laughter like breeze.

Resonating with Nautical Dreams

On a ship made of jelly, the captain's a clown,
He juggles the fish while the seagulls just frown.
With binoculars made out of soda cans,
He searches for pirates and forgotten plans.

The ship had a parrot with feathers so bright,
Who mimicked the captain with great delight.
'Yo ho!' she yelled, but forgot all the rest,
And ended up singing about a jesting quest.

In waters of custard, they danced on the foam,
Every wave was a chuckle, they felt right at home.
With mermaids who giggled and flippers that waved,
They tossed all their maps, for fun they were braved.

With laughter as currency, they bought salty air,
Trading goofy hats and their best funny stares.
So off sailed the crew, from dusk until dawn,
In the sea of their dreams, the joy carried on.

Luring Whispers Across the Oceans

In a sea full of butter, the sailors would glide,
With noodles for rigging, they'd take it in stride.
With a wink and a grin, they'd float on by night,
Fueled by the whispers of shimmering light.

A crab played the accordion, quite out of tune,
While the fish formed a chorus beneath the moon.
'Take us to fanciful places!' they'd call,
But the route led to nowhere; they giggled and sprawled.

On the shore, they found treasures wrapped in seaweed,
Like hats made of shells and candy to feed.
While the tides did their giggling, the crew danced with zeal,
The ocean a playground, a watery wheel.

With every splash, they'd erupt into cheers,
They sang as the dolphins popped up with their peers.
So luring the whispers that giggled and spun,
They embraced all the chaos, the warmth, and the fun.

Calling from the Depths of Memory

Once in a briny old bowl sat a fish,
Dreaming of currents and an odd, squid-like wish.
He called out to sailors with tales full of flair,
Of adventures in ruins and a bizarre chair.

With bubbles for speeches, he told of a queen,
Who knitted the waves, using threads from the scene.
She'd spin gold from kelp and weave laughter from foam,

In a castle of shells, where all creatures roam.

His tales echoed out like a soft flowing stream,
While the octopuses rolled their eyes, caught in a dream.
But the fish kept on spinning his yarns with a laugh,
'Join me, dear friends, for the best of all crafts!'

From the depths rose the echoes of chuckles so bright,
As sailors remembered their wild, fun-filled nights.
So if you hear laughter arise from below,
Just know it's a party, come join the show!

Song of the Mystic Waters

In waters deep where giggles float,
Fish wear hats and sing a note.
Octopuses juggle, oh what a sight,
Mermaids dance in the pale moonlight.

With bubbles rising, a tickle fest,
Turtles race—it's quite the quest!
Seahorses prance, wearing bright ties,
While seaweed sways, under the skies.

Clams tell jokes with shells so prim,
Snapping crustaceans learn to swim.
An eel jokes, "I'm not really neat!"
And everyone laughs, with fishy feet.

Where bubbles pop and laughter's near,
And salty tales bring boats to cheer.
So dive on in, let joy take flight,
In the giggling waves of the starry night.

Lure of the Coral Night

In coral gardens, all dressed in glee,
The starfish play as wild as can be.
They twirl in circles, flash their hues,
In a dance-off between yellow and blues.

Bubble-blowing fishes puff their chests,
Competing hard for the "Best Dressed!"
A clam yells loud, "I've got the bling!"
As briny breezes start to sing.

Anemones wiggle, ticklish and bright,
While crabby crabs giggle, "What's your plight?"
With corals chuckling in colors so bold,
They share a secret—a treasure of gold!

As starlight dapples the ocean floor,
The sea life giggles, asking for more.
Join the fun where the bubbles play,
And dance with creatures until break of day.

Siren's Lullaby

A tune is floating through the foam,
Where fish find peace, they feel at home.
Mermaids whisper, "Please don't snore!"
For the sea's so funny, you'll want to explore.

Jellyfish sway like pom-poms fair,
With glowing smiles, they light the air.
"Catch us if you can!" they tease with a grin,
As fishes giggle, "Let the games begin!"

Dolphins leap in rhythmic cheer,
Sculpting rainbows, oh so near.
Grouchy old turtles shuffle about,
Muttering, "What's this fuss about?"

But the waves chuckle as night descends,
With giggles and splashes where joy transcends.
So rest your eyes, let dreams take the lead,
In a watery world where laughter's the creed.

Chants of the Abyss

In the depths where shadows play,
Fish throw a party every day.
Glow-worms twist like disco lights,
While deep-sea creatures share their sights.

A fishy choir sings off-key,
With gurgles and bubbles, it's hard to see.
A clam plays drums with a heavy shell,
Making music that's quite a yell!

The anglerfish shows his flashy grin,
While playful squids indulge in spin.
"Come dance with us!" calls the seaweed tall,
While crabs do the cha-cha, both large and small.

In the abyss where laughter floats,
And all are friends in their playful coats.
So dive in deep, let joy persist,
For the ocean's laughter you cannot resist.